When To Use Wilderness Survival

The subject of this simulation (survival in a wilderness) is not the topic for learning. It merely provides an interesting, effective, and entertaining way to introduce problem solving and decision making to work teams or other groups. Nevertheless, the information learned about survival and decisions in emergency situations may also be of great benefit to the participants.

This simulation also provides immediate feedback to group members on how well they performed as a team. It can be used effectively in training for any of the following purposes:

Consensus Decision Making

This simulation will give a group or intact work team an opportunity to learn how to make decisions by consensus. This may be a new experience for some, because group decisions are frequently made by voting, trading, or negotiating. In many cases, however, a satisfactory decision can be reached only by consensus. If members of a group need to learn to make decisions by consensus, this simulation will not only give them practice, but will also reinforce the value of consensus decisions.

Synergistic Decision Making

This simulation explores the concept of synergy in regard to the outcomes of group decision making and also provides first-hand experience in synergistic decision making. It involves both interpersonal and problem-solving factors in reaching decisions.

General Problem Solving and Decision Making

In any effort to teach problem-solving or decision-making skills, this simulation provides an interesting and provocative situation for both individual and group tasks.

Comparing Individual Decisions with Team Decisions

This simulation will illustrate the benefit of using all the resources of a team rather than relying solely on the ability of one member to solve a problem or make a decision.

Teamwork

Participants will gain experience in interpersonal behaviors as they work together to arrive at decisions in this problem. It will give them an opportunity to examine the impact of interpersonal behaviors on team effectiveness and to support and confront one another in a nonthreatening environment.

Group Behavior

This simulation can be used to explore many aspects of group behavior, such as participation, leadership style, and communications.

WILDERNESS SURVIVAL

Leader's Manual

Pfeiffer
A Wiley Imprint
www.pfeiffer.com

This simulation is based on an activity submitted by Donald T. Simpson.

Published by Pfeiffer
A Wiley Imprint
989 Market Street, San Francisco, CA 94103-1741 www.pfeiffer.com

Pfeiffer books and products are available through most bookstores. To contact Pfeiffer directly call our Customer Care Department within the U.S. at 800-956-7739, outside the U.S. at 317-572-3986, or fax 317-572-4002.

Pfeiffer also publishes its books in a variety of electronic formats. Some content that appears in print may not be available in electronic books.

ISBN: 0-88390-241-9

Printed in the United States of America
Printing 10 9 8 7 6

Contents

Administration of Wilderness Survival

Major Goals

I. To teach the effectiveness of consensus-seeking behavior in task groups through comparative experiences with both individual decision making and group decision making.

II. To explore the concept of synergy with regard to the outcomes of group decision making.

Group Size

Four to nine participants (optimally, five to seven). Several groups may be directed simultaneously.

Time Required

Approximately 1½ hours.

Materials

I. Newsprint flip chart and felt-tipped markers.

II. A copy of the Wilderness Survival simulation for each participant.

III. A pencil for each participant.

IV. A poster or newsprint sheet showing the correct answers to the predicaments.

V. Charts for scoring (see step VII under "Process"). The charts should be prepared in advance, and scores will be recorded after participants complete the simulation.

Physical Setting

Lapboards or desk chairs are best for privacy in individual work. A table for each group is also needed. (The tables can be used for individual work, but the dynamics involved are likely to be different.)

Process

I. Distribute the Wilderness Survival simulation to participants. Explain that they should not break the seal until instructed to do so and that they should work independently during the first phase (i.e., "Your Task"). Ask them to read the instructions, and give them a signal to begin the task.

II. After thirteen minutes, give a two-minute warning. After the two minutes, instruct the participants to stop work.

III. Discuss consensus decision making (based on points from pages 9 and 10 of this manual) and ask participants to review the consensus guidelines on page 7 of their booklets. If the group consists of no more than seven people, the entire group should work together on the "Group's Task." Otherwise, divide the total group into subgroups, and identify each subgroup by name, number, or letter of the alphabet. Review the group-task instructions with the participants and ask the subgroups to begin the task.

IV. After about a half-hour, give the participants a two-minute warning and then—after two minutes—instruct them to stop work.

V. Explain that the participants will have a chance to discuss the rationale behind the answers but for the moment they should be concerned only with recording the "correct" answers. Post the correct answers but not the rationale.

Read aloud the following instructions and guide the participants through the scoring process:

> Write the letter (a, b, or c) that corresponds with the correct answer in the space provided under the heading "Correct Answer." Com-

pare the letters in "Your Answer" column and circle every letter that agrees with the correct answer. Total the number of circles and write the total in the appropriate space. This total represents your score.

Add the scores of all the members in your group and divide the total by the number of members in your group. The quotient should be worked out to one decimal place. This quotient is your group's average individual score. Write this average in the space provided.

Now circle all the correct letters in "Your Group's Answer" column, total the circles in that column, and write the total in the appropriate space. This number represents your group's score. Be ready to read your scores when asked to do so.

VI. Remind participants that the goal was not to learn how to survive in a wilderness and that the important part is the group process: that is, the teamwork, the consensus decisions, the synergistic decision making, the problem solving, and the interpersonal dynamics. Instruct the participants to break the seal and to read the rationale for the answers. Give them about ten minutes to discuss the rationale within the small groups.

VII. Post the following charts. Ask participants for scores and write the scores in the appropriate rectangles. Explain the synergy factor (based on points from page 10 of this manual) and help participants to determine whether or not their group experienced synergy. Instruct the participants to fill in the appropriate numbers on each chart on page 10 of their booklets.

BEFORE GROUP DISCUSSION

Group	Average Individual Score	Score of Most Accurate Individual
Example	7.2	9
1		
2		
3		
Average for all groups		

AFTER GROUP DISCUSSION

Group	Score for Group Consensus	Gain/Loss Over Average Individual	Gain/Loss Over Most Accurate Individual	Synergy*
Example	10	+2.8	+1	Yes
1				
2				
3				
Average for all groups				

*Synergy is defined as the consensus score higher than the highest individual score in the group.

VIII. Use the following questions to guide the participants through a discussion:

- What behaviors helped or hindered the consensus-seeking process?
- What patterns of decision making occurred?
- Who were the influential members? How were they influential?
- How did the group discover and use its information resources? Were these resources fully utilized?
- What are the implications of consensus-seeking and synergistic outcomes for intact task groups such as committees and staffs of organizations?
- What consequences might this process produce in the group's attitudes?

Variations

I. Process observers can be used to give feedback about group behavior and/or individual behavior.

II. Participants can give a copy of their individual decisions to the facilitator for scoring while they proceed with the group task.

Answers and Rationale

Here are the recommended courses of action for each of the predicaments in the Wilderness Survival simulation. These answers come from the comprehensive course on woodland survival taught by the Interpretive Service, Monroe County (New York) Parks Department. These responses are considered to be the best rules of thumb for most situations. Specific situations, however, might require other courses of action.

1. (a) **Call "help" loudly but in a low register.** Low tones carry farther, especially in dense woodland. There is a much better chance of being heard if you call loudly but in a low key. "Help" is a good word to use because it alerts others of your plight. Yelling, screaming, or whistling would not only be less effective but might be mistaken for a bird call.

2. (a) **Make a lot of noise with your feet.** Snakes do not like people and will usually do everything they can to get out of your way. Unless you surprise or corner a snake, there is a good chance that you will neither see nor come into contact with one. On the other hand, walking softly may bring you right on top of a snake. Some snakes feed at night, so that's not the best time to walk through snake country.

3. (c) **Put a bit of the plant on your lower lip for five minutes; if it seems all right, try a little.** The best approach, of course, is to eat only those plants that you recognize as safe. But when in doubt and very hungry, you may use the lip test. If the plant is poisonous, you will get a very unpleasant sensation on your lip. Red berries alone do not tell much about the plant's edibility (unless, of course, you recognize the plant by the berries). Birds do not have the same digestive systems as humans and do not provide a safe test.

4. (c) **Drink as much as you think you need when you need it.** The danger here is dehydration, and once the process starts, your liter of water will not do much to reverse it. Saving or rationing will not help, especially if you are lying unconscious somewhere from sunstroke or dehydration. So use the water as you need it, and be aware of your need to find a water source as soon as possible.

5. (c) **Dig in the stream bed at the outside of a bend.** This is the part of the river or stream that flows the fastest and is less silted, deepest, and the last to go dry.

6. (c) **Midway up the slope.** A sudden rain storm could turn the ravine into a raging torrent. This has happened to many campers and hikers before they had a chance to escape. The ridge line, on the other hand, increases your exposure to rain, wind, and lightning if a storm should break. The best location is on the slope.

7. (a) **Yellow.** A yellow flame indicates incomplete combustion and a strong possibility of carbon monoxide build-up. Each year many campers are killed by carbon-monoxide poisoning as they sleep or doze in tents, cabins, or other enclosed spaces.

8. (a) **Leave your boots and pack on.** Errors in fording streams are a major cause of fatal accidents. Sharp rocks or uneven footing demand that you keep your boots on. If your pack is fairly well balanced, wearing it will increase your stability in the swift current.

9. (b) **Across the stream in the direction you are walking.** Errors in facing the wrong way in fording a stream are the cause of many drownings. Facing upstream is the worst alternative; the current could push you back, and your pack would provide the unbalance to pull you over. You have the best stability when facing across the stream, keeping your eye on the exit point on the opposite bank.

10. (c) **In stocking feet.** This way you can pick your route to some degree, and you can feel where you are stepping. Normal hiking boots become slippery, and going barefoot offers your feet no protection at all.

11. (c) **Freeze, but be ready to back away slowly.** Sudden movement will probably startle the bear a lot more than your presence. If the bear is seeking some of your food, do not argue with him; let him forage and be on his way. Otherwise, back very slowly toward some refuge (trees, rock outcrop, etc.).

12. (b) **Put the batteries under your armpits to warm them, and then replace them in the flashlight.** Flashlight batteries lose much of their power and weak batteries run down faster in the cold. Warming the batteries, especially if they are already weak, will restore them for a while. You would normally avoid night travel, of course, unless you were in open country where you could use the stars for navigation. There are just too many obstacles (logs, branches, uneven ground, etc.) that could injure you; and a broken leg, injured eye, or twisted ankle would not help your plight. Once the sun sets, darkness falls quickly in wooded areas; it would usually be best to wait until daylight to travel.

Material for Discussion

Points made in the following paragraphs can be incorporated into explanations of consensus decision making and synergism.

Consensus

Decisions are made by consensus if all members in the group agree on the decision. This method should not be confused with voting, averaging, compromising, negotiating, or trading. The group must find a solution that every member can accept, even though some members may not be convinced that it is the best solution.

The ground rules may be summarized as follows:

1. No averaging.
2. No majority-rule voting.
3. No horse trading.

Following are some guidelines for arriving at a consensus decision:

1. Avoid arguing in order to win as individuals. What is "right" is the best collective judgment of the group as a whole.

2. Disagreements should be viewed as helpful rather than hindrances in reaching consensus. Group members should not give in just to reach an agreement. They should support only those solutions that they can truthfully accept.

3. Problems are solved best when individual group members accept responsibility for both listening and contributing, so that everyone is included in the decision.

4. Tension-reducing behaviors can be useful if meaningful conflict is not smoothed over prematurely.

5. Each member is responsible for monitoring the decision-making process and for initiating discussions about the process if it becomes ineffective.

6. The best results flow from a fusion of information, logic, and emotion. Value judgments about what is best include members' feelings about the data and the decision-making process.

Synergism

Synergy is the combined action of two or more agents that—when acting jointly—increase the effectiveness of one another and produce an outcome that is greater than the sum of the agents' outcomes when acting independently. Synergy can be expected when group members work together on Wilderness Survival. The combined knowledge, judgment, and problem-solving and decision-making abilities of the members generally produce a score that is higher (i.e., that is closer to the "correct" solution) than the average individual score. However, the fact that several people are meeting together and producing a solution does not necessarily mean that all their abilities will be utilized. Synergism is more likely to occur when the group follows the guidelines for consensus decision making.

A facilitator may well predict that a group will not produce a synergistic score if members of that group are carrying on more than one conversation at a time, if they keep interrupting one another, if they constantly jump from one subject to another, and/or if some of the members are not actively participating. To enjoy synergy, they must not only work toward producing the best solution, but they must also pay close attention to the process they are using to reach the solution.

Notes: